The

Educated at Glasgo ... nning writer and actor, An ... eatre, television and radio. She is also a published short story ... er and recently read one of her own short stories *Write Your Name Small* on radio 4. Her theatre plays include, *The White Bird Passes*, *Ashes to Ashes*, *Baba Yaga and the Magic Doll*, *Side Sea View*, *Jelly Babies*, *Waiting on One*, (LWT Award winner) *The Witches of Pollok*, *De Profundis*, *Bread Upon The Water*, *Retribution*, *Cracked* and *The Boy Beneath the Sea*. Her adaptation of *The Yellow on the Broom* was given its fifth sell-out production in 2005, this time at Perth Repertory Theatre. Her plays, many into third productions, have been produced by companies as diverse as Wildcat, The Tron, Theatre Workshop, Oran Mor, Cumbernauld, Perth, Communicado, The Byre, Borderline, Dundee Repertory Theatre and Dry Rain Theatre, Eire. Head hunted for television, she spent nine years writing for STV, BBC, Carlton, and Channel 4. Anne Downie lives and works in Glasgow.

fairplay press

The Witches of Pollok

by Anne Downie

fairplay press

First published by fairplay press, an imprint of Capercaillie Books Limited in 2007.

Registered office 1 Rutland Court, Edinburgh.

Printed in Poland.

A catalogue record for this book is available from the British Library.

ISBN 978-0-9551246-8-6

The publisher acknowledges support from the Scottish Arts Council towards the publication of this title.

Scottish Arts Council

Introduction

This play is based on historical fact insofar as five people were burned at the stake in 1677 for the alleged bewitching of Sir George Maxwell of Pollok. The person instrumental in their being brought to trial, was a stranger to the area named Janet Douglas, whose extraordinary powers puzzled the intellegentsia of the day.

Sir George was a learned and pious man who was fined 4000 pounds Scots for his covenanting sympathies. In 1677 the great fire of Glasgow destroyed 136 houses and shops and left 700 families homeless. Although the historical facts *provide* the bare bones of the play, I have woven together fact and fiction, inventing characters and incidents for dramatic purposes. It would be very easy to dismiss this tragic incident as yet another example of Scotland's unenviable record in witchhunting. Notwithstanding the fact that every age produces its scapegoats, the supernatural elements in this case however, even now, defy explanation.

When I visited the Glasgow Room in The Mitchell library for inspiration in the writing of a commissioned play for a contemporary piece of theatre, I came across an article in an old book of Glasgow tales about the bewitching of Sir George Maxwell in Pollok, Glasgow in 1676. Like the thousands of people who come from Scotland and all over the world to visit the famous Burrell Collection and Pollok House situated in Pollok Park, I had never heard of the alleged bewitching of Sir George Maxwell, the owner of Pollok House in 1676, which resulted in five of the people on his estate being burned at the stake for witchcraft. I was very intrigued, but put the idea aside for a couple of years as it did not fit the brief for my, then, current commission, a musical comedy.

In 1990 I was commissioned by Michael Boyd, now Artistic Director of the Royal Shakespeare Company, to write a play for the Tron Theatre, Glasgow, to celebrate Glasgow being chosen as the European City of Culture. My play, *Witches of Pollok* was the result.

In researching historical documents, council meetings, court records of the trial etc I was aware just how much the Scottish language has changed since the Union of 1707. In the period of the play, Scotland's official language was of course, distinctly different from our English neighbours. I have attempted to give a flavour of that in the dialogue in a way that is comprehensible to the modern reader. I found from the records that verb endings were different. It was common to end verbs like 'wanted in 'it' instead of 'ed' as they are today. If this is borne in mind, the meaning of verbs used in the play like 'forcit' 'showit' eg becomes apparent. However, I have also included a glossary of other Scots words used, many of which are still in common use throughout Scotland

I knew Scotland, historically, had a shocking reputation for witchcraft trials, but the main impetus for my play was the person known as Janet Douglas. The records gave only a tantalising glimpse of her character. What was her reason for pointing the finger at all these innocent souls? Was she, as some have said of Shakespeare's Iago, guilty of motiveless malignity. Or had physical and sexual abuse really soured her view of humanity? Michael Boyd who was directing the play, wrote back on receipt of my script saying he 'liked it very much. It reads like a real thriller-diller-sort of Arthur Miller meets Stephen King, resulting in a strong compelling piece of work'. He commissioned Oscar winner, Craig Armstrong to write a musical score for the piece ,which Craig played live throughout the performance. The Tron also produced an educational package for schools, for whom extra matinees were included.

I was keen to know what happened to Janet Douglas and through further research, found a letter from a minister in Edinburgh to a minister in Glasgow, saying that she had been 'dragged through the streets of Edinburgh before being deported to the colonies'. He wanted to know whether the Glasgow minister considered her a white,or a black witch, as many strange practices had been carried out in her name. I tried to find a record of her trial in the Edinburgh Law Court library, but there was none.The librarian reminded me that people were often deported to the colonies for very minor crimes. I've often wondered what havoc Janet Douglas wreaked there.

Anne Downie 2007

Characters

JANET DOUGLAS:	the accuser.
SIR GEORGE MAXWELL OF POLLOK:	a respected laird.
MARGARET MAXWELL:	his daughter.
LAURENCE MARTIN:	servant to Sir George.
JAMES DUNLOP:	servant to Sir George.
GILBERT PETTIGREW:	Margaret's suitor.
DR. BREMNER:	Physician to Sir George.
MARY ROBERTSON:	a sweetmeat seller.
ROB ROBERTSON:	her husband.
JENNIFER MATHIE STEWART:	Mary's mother.
JOHN STEWART:	Mary's brother.
ANNABIL STEWART:	her sister.
ALLAN GEDDES:	a showman.
THOMAS RAMSAY:	Commissioner for Witchcraft.
REVEREND REID	
REVEREND BELL	
GEORGE SINCLAIR:	Professor of Philosophy at the University of Glasgow and friend to Sir George.
MRS SINCLAIR:	his wife.
MARGARET JACKSON BESSIE WEIR MARGERY CRAIGE	tenants on Sir George's estate.
LORD ROSS:	a judge.
SIR PATRICK GAUSTON:	an advocate for the defence.
JOHN PRESTON:	an advocate for the prosecution.

ALE SELLER:	at the Glasgow Fair.
BETSIE:	stallholder at the Fair.
MR. SOUTAR	a Glasgow citizen visiting the fair.
MRS. SOUTAR	his wife.
TOWN GUARD	
ANDREW }	local guards.
LUDOWICK }	
GAOLER	
PEDLAR	
DRUMMER	
OTHERS:	stiltwalker, acrobat, wrestlers, clerk of court.

Production Notes

Double Casting

This play is structured in such a way that a company of ten actors and two musician or actors can play all parts.

Historical Note

The great fire of Glasgow in 1677 destroyed one hundred and thirty six houses and shops. Seven hundred families were left homeless. The centre of Glasgow including the tolbooth were set alight and prisoners including the laird of Kersland imprisoned for his part in the Pentland rising, escaped. Five people were burned at the stake in 1677 for the bewitching of Sir George Maxwell of Pollok.

Sources used in the play

Glasgow Fair in Olden Time
Fun of the Fair, Record and Mail Oct 1907
Glasgow Fair, The Glasgow Herald July 12th 1924
The Bell and the Tree, Edward Chisnall (Collins)
The Bewitching of Sir George Maxwell of Pollok, reprinted from the *Witches of Renfrew*, Paisley 1809
Rowan Tree and Red Thread

And numerous articles and items from the Glasgow room (Mitchell Library) and Pollokshaws library, Glasgow, for which many thanks to the library staff for their help and interest.

Scots words used in the play

ableeze	ablaze
afore	before
agin	against
ahint	behind
ain	own
airse	backside
amang	amongst
aroon	around
atween	between
aw	all
aye	always but also means yes
bairnies	children
baith	both
beyond oor ken	beyond our understanding
bide	stay
blether	someone who talks too much
bluid	blood
bonny fecht	a good fight
breeks	trousers
breist	breast
brither	brother
brocht	brought
buddy	person
ca' canny	watch your step
cairt	cart
cairter	carter
canna	can't
cheugh	tough
chynge	change
chynging	changing
cried fae the kirk	denounced in church
cuddies	donkeys or horses

daith	death
dicht	clean
dinna	don't
disnae ken her ain kin ony mair	doesn't know her own family any more
dochter	daughter
droons	drowns
dug	dog
dumbie	mute person
fair-grun'	fair-ground
feart	afraid
feenished	finished
feretellit	foretold
fower	four
fowk	folk
frae	from
freens	friends
gawn	going
gey	very
gey lang wey	a long way
gied	given
gies	gives
Glesca	Glasgow
guid	good
guid for nothing	good for nothing
hae	have
hale	whole
hame	home
haverin'	talking nonsense
haud ma wheesht	keep quiet
hermed	harmed
hogger	coarse stocking without a foot
hogh and goustie	hollow and eerie
hoochmagandie	fornication

hoor	whore, prostitute
hunners	hundreds
hunnert	hundred
inconveintis	trouble/punishment
intil	into
jile	jail
jougs	instrument of public punishment; hinged iron collar attached by chain to post and locked round offender's neck
joukin' aboot	running around
ken mair	know more
kens	knows
lang	long
lassie	girl
lugs	ears
maister	master
mannie	man
marrit	married
masel'	myself
merk	old Scottish currency
messin'	contemptuous term for a person
micht	might
mind	remember
mither	mother
mony	many
mooth	mouth
nae deid	not dead
neb	nose
nippit	niggardly
nye on	nearly
oorsels	ourselves
ower quickly	too quickly

paction	pact
passit awa	died
pey	pay
pit	put
pleesure	pleasure
puir	poor
pun	pound
relict	widow
richt	right
richt awa	right away
rin	run
sair	soor
scoorit	scoured
siller	silver
sowel	soul
spier	enquire
spiered	questioned
spikkin'	speaking
sterk nakit	stark naked
stervin	starving
stey	stay
straicht	straight
swayt	swayed
swelt up	swollen
tae	to
telt	told
tinks	tinkers
tinsell	loss
thrapple	throat
thocht	thought
toon	town
tuck of drum	drumbeat
twa	two

twinty	twenty
wattert doon	watered down
weel	well
weel markit	well defined
weel oot	well out
whaur	where
wheesht	be quiet
wheen	a good few
widnae herm	wouldn't harm
wifies	women
winna hae	wouldn't have
yase	use
yased that yin	used that one
yin	one
yince	once

Act 1

Scene 1

Glasgow Fair circa 1676. The audience should experience the smells, sights, sounds of the period. Two men wrestle bare-chested while the crowd shout encouragement. A stilt-walker strides backwards and forwards. A pedlar with brightly coloured ribbons on a tray peddles his wares.

MARY ROBERTSON moves through the crowd, a tray of sweetmeats round her neck, selling her wares; gingerbread, baps, treacle candy, honey biscuits etc. A juggler juggles. A fiddler and piper play for all they're worth. A curtained wheeled rostra is centre stage.

As the house lights fade, a sedan chair is carried on by JAMES DUNLOP and LAURENCE MARTIN, servants to SIR GEORGE MAXWELL OF POLLOK. They assist MARGARET MAXWELL, daughter of SIR GEORGE, to alight. She is a spirited determined girl of around eighteen years of age.

LAURENCE: Ca' canny, Miss Margaret! You'll ruin your shoes!

JAMES is an older retainer who has known MARGARET since she was a baby . . . and tends to be over protective towards her.

JAMES: Dinna leave oor side noo Mistress. This is nae place for a lady!

MARGARET: **(impatiently)** Oh, for goodness sake, wheesht! You're like twa cluckin' hens! I've aye wantit to see the Fair an' see it I will!

LAURENCE: There are some gey rough fowk around here Miss! You . . .

MARGARET: Nonsense. I've read all about it. They say Glasgow has the best run fair in the hale o' Scotland.

As she goes to rush off.

JAMES: Come back here Miss Margaret. If onything happint to ye, I'd be held responsible.

MARGARET: You're releivit of all responsibility, James. It was me forcit you to come here.

LAURENCE: Bide close by oor side Mistress. It's hoachin wi thieves and drunks.

MARGARET: Well it'll make a nice change fae nippit auld ministers o' the kirk and lang windit gentlemen o' the law.

JAMES: **(reprovingly)** Your sister wis dain her best to entertain ye Mistress. It's no often she gets the chance to show ye off to Glesca society.

MARGARET: **(sarcastically)** If that's Glasgow society, then Polloktoon should hae Royal aspirations! If I had to sit through yin mair o' those interminable dinners, ma lugs would hae drappit aff fae sheer boredom!

JAMES: Mind noo,we canny bide here lang. Mistress Marion will hae the hale hoose oot lookin' for ye.

MARGARET: Dinna fash, James. I telt her I was payin' a charitable call for faither. **(Chuckles.)** Oor Marian thinks everyone is as honest as herself.

The PEDLAR approaches.

PEDLAR: Ribbons for the fine lady.

LAURENCE: Awa' wi ye!

MARGARET: Tch tch! Mind your manners, Laurence. I'll hae the blue yin. **(Hands him a coin.)**

PEDLAR: Guid health tae wear it mistress . . .

He is interrupted by a roll of drums. A drummer appears in front of the curtained rostra.

DRUMMER: If you want your future foretellit and your past to be revealit. Then gather roon yin an aw.

MARGARET: **(moving nearer)** Come on! I want to hear this!

The crowd gather round the rostra. The drummer gives another roll on the drums. ALAN GEDDES appears with a flourish, dressed in a flashy showman's coat. He has a brash confidence about him coupled with an inherent seediness.

GEDDES: **(loudly)** Ladies and gentlemen . . . if there be any amang ye . . .

Crowd Jeer.

LAURENCE: Bliddy cheek! Beggin' your pardon, Mistress!

GEDDES: Freens . . . ahint this curtain is someone who will amaze and astound ye. In aw ma years comin to the great Fair o' Glesca I hae showit ye mony wonders.

FIRST HECKLER: **(male)** Aye, like your three heidit coo!

SECOND HECKLER: **(his wife)** An' your beardit bairnies!

GEDDES: **(raises his hand for silence)** Ladies and gentlemen . . . what you are about to witness defies any description. You are about to come face to face wi someone whose supreme powers canny be explainit.

SECOND HECKLER: **(laughs)** It's King Cherlie!

Another drum roll sounds.

GEDDES: Freens . . . I give you the yin . . . the only . . . Janet Douglas!!

There is a distant rumble of thunder . . . JANET DOUGLAS steps through the curtains. She is a young girl whose age would be difficult to pinpoint. She has a composure about her that seems unnatural in one so young, coupled with an air of one who seems distanced from her surroundings.

FIRST HECKLER: She hasnae got twa heids. Hey! **(To JANET.)** Whit's sae special aboot you?

GEDDES: Sir, she canny answer ye. The Lord in His wisdom has made her a dumbie . . . wi' nae power o' verbal communication. **(Sympathetic murmurings from the crowd.)** Save your sympathy freens . . . Janet here has nae need for pity, for Mother Nature has compensated twinty times ower. You see afore ye nae ordinary lass,but yin who is blessit with the most extraordinary powers.

SECOND HECKLER: Oh aye, lets see them!

MARY ROBERTSON the sweetmeat seller passes around the crowd.

MARY: A wee bit sweetie, maam . . . sir? It's gawn tae be a lang nicht.

GEDDES: Madam! Wid ye kindly refrain frae hawkin your wares while I'm aboot ma business.

MARY: It's a free country!

FIRST HECKLER: Thats nae whit Cherlie says!

MARY: Anyway you dinna own the hale fair-grun'.

GEDDES: **(angry)** I'll speak tae you later Mary Robertson!

MARY: **(sexily)** Ohh . . . I canna wait!

Laughter from crowd. GEDDES holds his hand up and signals to the drummer.

GEDDES: Ladies and Gentlemen . . . I'm not going to try and explain this lassie's powers. I will merely demonstrate them. I would like a volunteer to pass up any object of a personal nature . . . Janet here will then astound you by revealing information known only by its owner. C'mon, you sir . . . who's been doin aw the shoutin'. Hae you an object for us?

The FIRST HECKLER passes up a crumpled handkerchief. GEDDES holds it between his fingers as if fearing contamination.

GEDDES: I won't deduce the obvious frae this. I'll leave this to our expert . . . Friends . . . prepare to witness a miracle. This lassie canna speak but she has the power tae transfer thought. I will become the instrument o' Janet's speech. Her thoughts will travel from her mind to ma mooth. I have promised you a miracle, ladies and gentlemen and Alan Geddes always keeps his word . . . but I must request a perfect silence, if you please.

Drum roll.

JANET shuts her eyes as does GEDDES. GEDDES holds the handkerchief up in one hand and takes JANET's hand in his other. There is a pause.

GEDDES: William Soutar, to whom this kerchief belongs, you are having fornicating relations with one who is not your wife.

MR. SOUTER (the first heckler) looks startled.

MRS. SOUTAR: Whit! Lets hear more!

GEDDES: This adulterous relationship has continuit these twa months past. **(MR. SOUTER looks extremely uncomfortable.)** You have giftit this woman many tokens o' your love. Includit in these, be siller, lace, sweetmeats an' locks o' your own hair.

MRS. SOUTAR grabs her husband by the hair furiously.

MRS. SOUTAR: I'll gie ye some mair hair for your hoor, ya messin! I'll tear oot your hale heid!

MR. SOUTAR breaks free and runs off pursued by his angry wife.

MRS. SOUTAR: Come back ya fornicatin swine ye!

The crowd laugh.

GEDDES: May we have have another object, ladies and gentlemen . . . I'm offerin' ye the opportunity o' a lifetime. A chance to hae your future foretellit. Come on . . . dinna be feart!

MARGARET removes a comb from her hair.

MARGARET: Here Laurence, give him this.

LAURENCE: Are ye sure, Miss Margaret?

JAMES: Best to leave these queer fowk alane.

LAURENCE: Aye!

MARGARET Do you work for ma faither or don't you?

LAURENCE: Yes, but . . .

MARGARET: Then do as your telt!

LAURENCE pushes through the crowd to the front.

LAURENCE: Here ma mannie. **(Hands up the comb to GEDDES.)** And mind, I want that back!

GEDDES: **(sarcastically)** Widnae hae thought it wis your colour sir.

Crowd laugh.

Are ye ready Janet?

JANET nods and holds up the comb as before. Drum roll as GEDDES holds her free hand.

GEDDES: Now . . . yes . . . the owner of this object is a young lady of quality. She is paying a visit to our fair town of Glasgow. She bides in Polloktoon, and . . . yes . . . is the daughter of Sir George Maxwell of Pollok. She . . . **(He breaks off holding his head as if in pain. JANET mirrors his actions.)** She . . . oh . . . oh . . .

He writhes as if in agony. The crowd begin to mutter in alarm. MARGARET pushes her way to the front.

JAMES: **(afraid)** Stay away Miss Margaret!

MARGARET: **(to GEDDES)** What is it you see? I want to know?

GEDDES: It's your faither . . . oh . . .

He doubles over in pain holding his side. JANET stands stock still, staring fixedly ahead in a trance like state.

MARGARET: **(urgently)** Whit aboot my faither? Tell me . . .

GEDDES: You must leave here at once! He is calling for you! He has been struckit doon. **(Writhes.)** Oh . . . the pain. I feel his torment! Go . . . go hame at once before the life leaves his wrackit body!

He drops to the ground and lies motionless. JANET continues to stare ahead.

MGT: **(distraught)** Oh . . . Father, Father . . . Laurence!

LAURENCE: **(puts arm around her)** It's a' richt Miss Margaret. It's just trickery.

MGT: Take me back to Pollktoon. Faither's sick . . . he needs me.

JAMES: We'll get richt back noo Miss.

She hurries over to the sedan escorted by LAURENCE and JAMES.

JAMES: Let's get the hell oota here!

They leave quickly.

The CROWD begin to whisper and mutter to themselves. They are fearful. Their mutterings should increase in volume to become a frightened, then angry chorus.

CROWD: Who is she?
Is it a trick?
How does she dae it?
It canny be!
How does she dae it?
It's devils work . . .
Devils work!!

They start to shout at JANET who has emerged from her trance and looks afraid.

Sister of Satan, awa wi' you . . .
Sister of Satan *awa*!

GEDDES gets to his feet, shakily. He sees that the crowd are beginning to move off.

GEDDES: Now ladies and gentlemen. I will pass amang ye. Please be generous in your appreciation.

WOMAN: **(shacking her fist)** It's the gaol ye should be gettin'.

Crowd move away.

GEDDES: Freens . . . it's only a bit o' fun. Come back . . .

MAN: You should be cried frae the Kirk!

WOMAN: Reportit to the cooncil!

MAN: **(as he leaves)** Burnt at the stake!!

The CROWD exit.

GEDDES seizes JANET angrily.

GEDDES: Ye treacherous wee bitch! Why did ye force me to speak thae things. I've been guid to ye. Gied ye food an' shelter . . . an' you've brocht nothin' but trouble in return.

JANET tries to indicate that she couldn't help it.

GEDDES: Dinna come the innocent wi' me. Ye ken exactly whit your dain'! Frightnin' awa ma customers. Well b'God I'll gie *you* somethin' to be feart frae! **(He pushes her to the ground and unbuckles his leather belt.)** You're evil! Ye ken that, and evil doers deserve punishment. It says so in the holy scripture. Well I'm goin tae perform a Christian act. Do you hear me! I'm goin' tae beat the Devil oot o' your hide!

MARY ROBERTSON reappears and attempts to come between them.

MARY: You'll dae nae such thing. Leave the lass alane!

GEDDES: **(angry)** This is nane o' your business, woman. It's atween me an' ma employee.

MARY: I'm makin it mine, Geddes! Pit that belt doon!

GEDDES pushes her away and she falls to the ground.

GEDDES: I'm warnin' you! Keep your neb oot o' it or I'll start on you.

MARY picks herself up and runs off. GEDDES turns back to JANET, winding his belt round his hand.

GEDDES: I've nae earnit yin merk wi your cairry on. I telt ye te gie only guid news to ma customers. You're goin to regret playing false wi' me! **(She backs off terrified.)** I dinna ken wha you really are but I'm warnin' ye . . . if you hae ony freens they'll no' be able to recognise ye when I'm feenished!

MARY ROBERTSON enters with a stallholder bearing a pike. She points to GEDDES.

MARY: That's him!

STALLHOLDER: Pit that belt doon Geddes and pick on someone your ain size.

GEDDES: Awa an sell your wattert-doon ale. You've nae authority here!

STALLHOLDER: Oh, but I have. The dean o' crafts ordit me to keep the peace here. **(He grabs GEDDES.)** It's the stocks for you ma mannie. You can cool your heels and await the magistrates pleesure!

GEDDES: **(to JANET . . . shouts)** I'll get you! I'm warnin' you. You better bide weel oot ma road!

STALLHOLDER: Move your airse, Geddes or you'll hae the point o' this up it!

JANET falls to the ground weeping. MARY puts her arm round her comfortingly.

MARY: There . . . there, lass. Dinna pey him ony heed. He's an auld blether breeks. You rin awa hame noo . . . and keep weel oot the road when he's releasit.

JANET tries to indicate that she's nowhere to go.

MARY: **(puzzled)** Whit d'ye mean? I dinna ken whit you're trying to tell me.

JANET tries again in dumb show.

MARY: Oh . . . I see . . . you've naewhere to go. I forgot you were lodgit wi' Geddes. Weel we cannae hae you wanderin the toon. Glesca can be a bit on the wild side roon fair time . . . no that onybody in the toon wid harm ye but ye get aw sorts o' thiefs an tinks joukin' aboot. You best come hame wi' me. It's no a castle mind ye, but ye'll be safe.

JANET takes her hands and kisses them. MARY is embarrassed by this show of gratitude.

MARY: Awa' wi' ye! There's nae need for that. You'd dae the same for me. Come on . . . ma mannie'll think I've run awa wi a pedlar if I dinna get a move on. **(Laughs. As they leave.)** No that I huvnae considered it. He can be a gey tetchy auld fart at times!

Scene 2

Pollok house. The home of SIR GEORGE MAXWELL OF POLLOK. SIR GEORGE is lying in bed attended by his physician, DOCTOR BREMNER. MARGARET rushes in.

MARGARET: Father . . . Father.

The physician puts his finger to his lips and draws her aside.

MARGARET: **(anxiously.)** How is he Doctor?

DR. BREMNER: Not too well, Miss Margaret. The fever is ower high.

MARGARET: I telt him no to visit Paisley last week. They say there's still plague in that toon.

DR. BREMNER: It's no' the plague, Mistress.

MARGARET: Then whit ails him?

DR. BREMNER: He complains that his left side is bein' stabbit. The pain is takin a' his strength away.

MARGARET: What can you do for him? Surely . . .

DR. BREMNER: I gave him some physic last night . . . but to no avail.

MARGARET: Hae you opened a vein?

DR. BREMNER: I have, lass. For I feared he had a pleurisy.

MARGARET: And did it hae any effect?

DR. BREMNER: I'm afraid not m'dear. The pain has increasit and his fever continues to rise.

MARGARET: But there must be something else you can do, surely?

DR. BREMNER: **(holding her hands)** I hae usit aw ma skill, Miss Margaret. It's in the Lord's hands noo.

MARGARET: **(distressed)** May I see him, Doctor?

DR. BREMNER: Aye, lass . . . but dinna tire him. He's in sair need o' aw his strength.

MARGARET crosses to the bed, where SIR GEORGE . . . a man in his late fifties lies, eyes closed . . . with a grey pallor.

MARGARET: Father . . . Father . . . can you hear me?

He opens his eyes and turns his head with a great deal of effort.

SIR GEORGE: **(weakly)** Margaret . . . is that you?

MARGARET: It is Father. I'm here.

SIR GEORGE: Thank the guid Lord. I was feart I'd quit this world without takin' leave o' you.

MARGARET: **(tearfully)** Dinna talk like that Father . . . you canna leave us.

SIR GEORGE: You better contact your brother and sisters . . . ohhh . . .

He writhes in pain.

MARGARET: **(calling)** Doctor! Doctor Bremner!

DR. BREMNER and JAMES rush in.

DR. BREMNER: Help me lift him up, James.

They raise him up. DR. BREMNER puts a glass to his lips.

DR. BREMNER: Take some more laudanum, Sir George . . . twill ease the pain.

MARGARET starts to cry as SIR GEORGE's face is contorted with pain.

JAMES: It would be best if you leave him Miss Margaret. He needs rest and prayer.

MARGARET: **(crying)** Oh, Father Father.

JAMES: **(calling out)** Laurence!

As LAURENCE appears he beckons him to take MARGARET away.

LAURENCE: Come on, Miss Margaret . . . leave it to the Doctor. He kens best whit to dae.

MARGARET: **(kissing SIR GEORGE)** Father . . . father . . . d'you hear me. I'll be outside the door if you need me. I love you Father.

LAURENCE leads her away. JAMES and DR. BREMNER help SIR GEORGE to lie down. JAMES gets down on his knees by the bed and starts to pray.

Fade.

Scene 3

In the home of MARY ROBERTSON, the sweetmeat seller. She and her husband ROB, are in each others arms. Throughout the scene, we see JANET DOUGLAS sitting in

the half light, in what should seem like another room, ideally on another level. The idea of her being an all seeing presence should be created. As ROB and MARY become more passionate, JANET, obviously disturbed, puts her hands over her ears, shuts her eyes, trying to blot them out.

MARY pushes him away as he tries to tear off her clothes.

MARY: Stop it! She'll hear you!

ROB: **(annoyed)** Why did ye bring her back here in the first place? Hae I no' enough mooths tae feed?

MARY: I couldnae leave her tae roam the streets could I?

ROB: That's why we hae an almshoose in Glesca.

MARY: She's scarcely mair than oor Annabil's age. I widnae pit the dug in that place. Some o' them there wid hae it for their supper.

ROB: Weel . . . whit aboot her ain folk? Hae ye asked her aboot them?

MARY: I tried but she didnae seem to ken whit I wis on aboot.

ROB: Weel . . . she'll hae to move on, if whit your brother says is true and your mother's comin' to bide.

MARY: Hae you ony reason to doubt him?

ROB: I doot every word that comes oot your John's mooth. He talks oot his airse hauf the time.

MARY: **(protesting)** That's no fair, Rab. Mother says he's settled doon since he startit at the Shamy mill.

ROB: No afore time! He's your mother's heart roastit!

MARY: **(sighing)** Aye! I'm glad she an' Annabil are comin'. It'll dae them guid to get awa fae Polloktoon for a whilie.

ROB: Aye, time spent awa fae your John wid be a tonic tae onybuddy. He's tuppence aff the merk, that yin!

MARY: Weel he seems to be bucklin' doon at the skinnin'.

ROB: I hope he's keepin weel oot the wey o' Sir George Maxwell.

MARY: Ach that's aw blown ower now. Sure he hid oot in the Darnley for nye on a year.

ROB: Dinna you believe it. The gentry hae lang memories. It's weel seeing Sir George is poorly, or that brother o' yours wid be in the jile.

MARY: **(alarmed)** Who says he's poorly?

ROB: Your John. Says he's been ill this week past.

MARY: **(fearful)** Oh no!

ROB: Whit's wrang wi' you? You look as if you've seen a ghost.

MARY: It's come true! It wisnae a trick.

ROB: Whit are you bletherin aboot?

MARY: **(clutching him fearfully)** She prophesied it. She kent Sir George Maxwell wis takin' poorly.

ROB: Who?

MARY: Janet . . . **(Alarmed.)** I thocht it wis Alan Geddes up to his usual tricks. **(Urgently.)** Rob . . . I want her oot o' here!

ROB: Thank God! At last you're talkin' sense! That's whit I've been trying to tell ye all night. She maks ma flesh creep! Looks at ye as if she can see your very soul. **(Moves.)** I'll tell her to get the hell oota here, richt noo.

MARY: **(restraining him)** No . . . no . . . leave her to the morning. We canna pit her oot in the middle o the night.

ROB: Who canna! We've done mair than oor Christian duty. She's been here a week an' hasnae offert a penny for her keep.

MARY: She hasnae got it to offer.

ROB: Weel she could get aff her backside and look for work. There's plenty to be had for those that want it!

MARY: Be fair. She's mair than paid her way. She's oor clothes near washit awa, and the hoose has been scoorit fae top tae bottom.

ROB: Weel I'll no be sorry to see the back o' her. I'm nae yin for flights o' fancy but that lassie gies me a strange feelin'.

MARY: **(afraid)** Whit kind o' feelin?

ROB: I cannae pit ma finger oan it . . . it's as if . . . as if . . . somebody had steppit oan ma grave!

The light goes out on JANET who disappears from view. MARY looks terrified.

ROB: Look, enough blethers! I'll awa an tell her she can shift her airse the morn.

MARY: No, no let me do it. We dinna want tae pit her agin us!

ROB: I winna!

MARY: **(firmly)** Leave it tae me, I said. You're nae exactly kent for your diplomacy.

ROB: Ach. **(Turns away.)** Please yoursel'!

MARY leaves the room. ROB lights a candle from the tinderbox.

MARY returns. He turns, surprised.

ROB: Bi' Goad . . . That didnae tak long.

MARY: **(surprised)** She's awa!

ROB: Awa where?

MARY: I dinna ken. She's taken her bits an' pieces and clearit awa. She's left this.

Hands him a letter.

ROB: I didnae ken she could write. She never let oan.

MARY: Whit's it say?

He crosses to the candle and reads by its light.

ROB: 'I must go where I'm needed.'

MARY: Is that aw?

ROB: Aye . . . no even a bye your leave or a thank you.

MARY: That's gey odd!

ROB: Guid riddance . . . that's whit I say. Noo I kin hae a wee bit **(grabs her)** hoochmagandie withoot bein' telt tae haud ma wheesht.

He cuddles her. MARY's face is to the audience. It is apparent that she is preoccupied and fearful.

Crossfade.

Scene 4

The great hall of Pollok. The stage fills up with estate workers, including JENNY MATHIE, (mother of MARY

ROBERTSON) and JENNY's younger daughter ANNABIL . . . aged fourteen. JENNY is sixty years of age and a strong woman who's not had an easy life.

JAMES is addressing the assembled workers who have gathered to enquire after SIR GEORGE's health. The latter is their employer. There is a deference paid to all associated with him at the 'big house'.

JAMES: I hae telt Miss Margaret that you're here. She'll be doon tae see you richt awa.

JENNY: How is the Laird?

JAMES: Richt poorly I'm afraid. He's had another nicht wrackit wi' pain and distemper. **(Sympathetic murmurings from workers.)** He is however puttin' up a bonny fecht. He . . . **(He breaks off as MARGARET enters.)** Ah, Miss Margaret . . . some o' Sir George's estate workers are here tae spier aboot his health. **(Indicates JENNY.)** You ken the Widow Mathie, wife o' Mr Stewart, the late under Miller o' the Shaw-mill and her dochter Annabil?

MARGARET: I dae indeed. My faither spoke highly o' your late husband Mistress Stewart. A richt good worker by aw accounts.

JENNY: **(drily)** Aye . . . ower guid Miss Margaret. That's why he's in the Shaws cemetery the day. I hope to God your puir faither'll no be joinin' him.

MARGARET: **(taken aback)** Amen to that Mistress. I'd like to thank you for coming here today . . . and you Hector and Douglas. I ken how busy you all are. My faither and the faimily appreciate aw your kind wishes and messages o' sympathy. Aw we can do is pray for Divine intervention on his behalf . . . I fear it's only his stubborn spirit that's keepit him here. His sufferin' is . . .

She is interrupted by LAURENCE who bursts in excitedly, clutching a letter.

LAURENCE: Excuse me Miss Margaret, but I hae an urgent message for ye. **(Hands her the letter.)** It's frae her!

MARGARET: Who?

LAURENCE: She's here to see you.

MARGARET opens the letter and reads.

MARGARET: What does this mean? This woman claims she can cure my faither.

LAURENCE: **(excitedly)** She kens whit ails him, she says.

MARGARET: Who is this from? There's nae signature.

LAURENCE: It's frae her, Miss Margaret. The dumbie fae Glesca Fair. Her that foretellit your father's illness.

MARGARET: She's here?

LAURENCE: Aye Mistress . . . ootside.

MARGARET: **(urgently)** Show her in!

LAURENCE exits.

JAMES: **(fearfully)** Ca' canny . . . Miss Margaret. How does she ken these things?

MARGARET: I dinna understand it either James, but I'll talk tae anyone wha says they can help faither.

LAURENCE returns with JANET. He propels her forward. She crosses to MARGARET and stares into her face . . . grabs her hands and starts to breathe heavily . . . then her head begins to circle in a trance-like state.

The others stand back and mutter fearfully.

JAMES: **(afraid)** Keep awa Mistress!

MARGARET: Quiet James . . . she's trying to tell me something!

JANET is mouthing trying to produce a sound. With a great effort she manages to produce a weird animal like sound. She keeps up a sustained note. She suddenly stops and says one word loudly and clearly.

JANET: Witchcraft!

LAURENCE: She can talk!

MARGARET: **(urgently)** What are you saying? Someone has bewitchit my faither?

JANET nods.

MARGARET: Do you ken who?

JANET nods again.

MARGARET: Tell me . . . in God's name who has causit this pain.

JAMES: Give us a name. We need a name.

JANET utters the animal sound even more loudly on a high pitched eerie note. The others fall back as she spins round she stops suddenly in her tracks with arm outstretched and finger pointing straight at JENNY MATHIE.

MARGARET: Jennifer Mathie! Is she the one?

JANET nods agitatedly.

JENNY: **(confused)** Whit's goin' on? Whit's she sayin'?

JAMES: **(accusingly)** That you're a witch, Jennifer Mathie.

JENNY: **(indignantly)** She's haverin'! The lassie's mad! She disnae ken whit she's spikkin' aboot.

LAURENCE: **(threateningly)** Whit have you done to Sir George?

JENNY: Me? Nothin' . . . I've nothin' agin the laird. He's aye been guid to me. I'd never wish him ill.

HECTOR: That's nae whit I've heard!

MARGARET: Whit have you heard? Speak up mannie! Dinna be feart!

HECTOR: She cursit the laird because he threatened that guid for nothin' son o' hers.

MARGARET: Who's her son?

HECTOR: John Stewart.

JAMES: That rogue!

MARGARET: Whit's this aw aboot James? Is there any truth in it? Did my faither threaten her son?

JAMES: Nae withoot cause Miss Margaret. That rascal brokit into Sir George's orchards and strippit near every tree till it wis sterk nakit.

LAURENCE: Aye an' then wis brass neckit enough tae sell the laird's apples fae a cairt in the Shaws.

MARGARET: An' did faither hae him punishit or what?

JAMES: The fly young tyke took wing, Mistress . . . flew awa to the Darnley last I heard. Sir George only threatened him wi' the micht o' the law if he returnit.

LAURENCE: An' he was quite within his richts to dae so.

MARGARET turns to JENNY angrily.

MARGARET: An was this reason tae bewitch him?

JENNY: **(agitated)** I tell you the dumbie's lying! I widnae ken how tae bewitch even if I wantit to!

LAURENCE: **(accusingly)** And did you want to Jenny Mathie? You were angry at the laird for threatenin' your son, were you no'?

JENNY: I was upset that I didnae see oor John for nye on a year but I never hermed Sir George . . . I swear it!

JAMES: **(to ANNABIL)** An' whit do you ken aboot this business, lass?

JENNY: **(sharply)** Keep ma dochter oot o this. She's but a bairn. She kens nae mair than me.

LAURENCE: She's got a guid Scots tongue in her heid . . . let her yase it.

JAMES: **(gently)** Annabil . . . whit can ye tell us lass.

ANNABIL: **(terrified)** I . . . I ken nothin' . . . honest, maister.

JANET makes the terrifying sound again at points at ANNABIL accusingly.

JANET: Witchcraft!

JENNY grabs her in fury.

JENNY: You lyin' bitch! I'll gie ye witchcraft!

LAURENCE and JAMES restrain her. ANNABIL weeps.

MARGARET: These are serious charges Janet Douglas. You canny make accusations withoot proof.

JANET takes a piece of paper from her pocket and hands it to MARGARET.

MARGARET: Whit's this drawin'? Can ye mak anything o' this James?

JAMES: **(studying it)** Looks like the plan o' a hoose Miss. See the fire-place is weel markit.

MARGARET: Whose house is this Janet?

JANET points to JENNY MATHIE then back to the paper indicating they must go there.

LAURENCE: She's tellin' us to go there.

JAMES: Whit's there? Will we find proof there o' witches work.

JANET takes the paper held by MARGARET and turns it over.

MARGARET: It's a drawing . . . of a doll.

LAURENCE: Look Mistress! It's got pins in its side!

MARGARET: **(horrified)** Oh, my God! Is that what's happint to faither?

JANET nods vigorously. The rest recite in chorus circling JENNY and ANNABIL accusingly.

ALL: Sisters of Satan.
Daughters of Beelzebub . . . confess!
Free yourself from the clutches of Lucifer.
Repent! Repent! *Repent*!

ANNABIL clutches her mother's hand in absolute terror.

JENNY: It's a lie! I ken nothin aboot this. D'you hear me!

JANET grabs LAURENCE and JAMES by the hand and indicates that she wants them to go with her.

MARGARET: Do as she says, James. Go with her to Jenny Mathie's house. Find out the truth o' the matter.

JAMES: **(uneasily)** I dinna like meddlin' in these maitters. We should report this to the Privy Cooncil.

MARGARET: Faither will die if we dinna tak' action richt noo James.

JAMES: I winna hae that on ma conscience. Richt Laurence, we'll go straicht away. You come wi' us Janet, if you please.

JENNY: You can aw come. I've nothin' to hide. You'll find oot for yoursel who is the liar here.

They leave. Only MARGARET is left onstage. She hears a cry of pain coming from SIR GEORGE.

MARGARET: **(tearfully)** Oh, faither . . . hold on! I'm comin'!

Scene 5

MARY ROBERTSON's house in Glasgow. MARY runs in calling hysterically.

MARY: Rob . . . Rob . . . whaur are ye?

ROB enters quickly.

ROB: Whit's wrang? Is the hoose burnit doon or whit?

MARY: **(sobbing)** Oh . . . Rob! Rob.

ROB: Calm doon Mary . . . tell me whit's happint.

MARY: It's Mother!

ROB: Whit aboot her? **(Concerned.)** She's no passit awa has she?

MARY: She's been arrestit!

ROB: Arrestit? . . . For whit?

MARY: **(sobbing)** Witchcraft!

ROB: Witchcraft! They're haverin'. Wha telt ye this?

MARY: Willie Erskine.

ROB: The cairter?

MARY: Aye . . . he was bringing a load through fae Polloktoun. Says ma brither telt him. Askit him tae let me know.

ROB: Are ye sure this isnae anither o' your brithers havers.

MARY: He widna fool aboot somethin' like this. Says ma mither's in the jail in Paisley.

ROB: God's bluid!

MARY: **(urgently)** I'll hae tae go to her.

ROB: Ye canna go tae Paisley. They've got the pestilence there.

MARY: No . . . Willie says its aw clearit up. He made a delivery there last week.

ROB: It's a gey lang wey.

MARY: I'll need tae go. **(Tearfully.)** God only kens whit they're dain to her. Yince a body's arrestit for witchcraft they'll day onythin' to mak them confess.

ROB: They'll never get your mither tae confess tae somethin's she's nae knowledge o'. She's a gey stubborn auld bird!

MARY: **(anguished)** That's whit I'm feart fae. They'll torture her! They hae weys tae break onybuddy's spirit! **(Cries.)**

ROB: There, there lass. **(Puts his arm round her.)** Dinna fash! I'll mak aw the arrangements.

Scene 6

We hear a piercing scream. Lights up on JENNY MATHIE who is manacled to the wall. A burly GAOLER stands over her. The COMMISSIONER for Witchcraft gestures him to stand aside. We can see that JENNY MATHIE is in great distress. The REVEREND REID mouths a silent prayer throughout the proceedings.

COMMISSIONER: Weel, Jennifer Mathie . . . are you ready to confess to your paction wi' Satan? You only hae to say the word and my freen here will leave you in peace.

JENNY: **(defiantly through the pain)** Peace to be burnit at the stake. That's whit you mean.

COMMISSIONER: Come, come, Jenny we widna be sae hasty. We hae mony fair trials for you to undergo afore we reachit that happy release.

JENNY: I ken aboot your 'fair trials'. They aye have the same conclusion.

REVD.REID: Confess and repent Jennifer Mathie. It's not too late. Only The Lord can stop Satan's fury and hinder him in his design. Free yourself from The devil's yoke.

JENNY: **(wearily)** I've done nothin'. How lang dae I hae to keep tellin' you that?

COMMISSIONER: Till you hae a chynge o' heart and speak the truth for yince.

JENNY: I've telt ye. I'm innocent.

COMMISSIONER: **(thrusting a wax doll in front of her)** Then how dae you explainit this awa?

JENNY: I ken nothin' o' this.

COMMISSIONER: Then how would it come to be hidden awa in a secret place ahint your fireplace.

JENNY: **(wearily)** I've telt ye a hunnert times. It was the deed o' the dumb girl. She pit it there.

COMMISSIONER: Sir George's twa servants James Dunlop and Laurence Martin . . . honest men baith . . . swearit on oath, on oath, mind ye, that the dumb lass, Janet Douglas, was naewhere near your fireplace. Are you sayin' they're liars tae?

JENNY: She pit it there I tell ye!

COMMISSIONER: Perhaps you can tell us how.

JENNY: I dinna ken. She has powers I canna understand. It's her you should be questionin' nae me. I widnae herm Sir George!

COMMISSIONER: Then how do you explain his miraculous recovery since we removit the pins frae this wax doll found in your dwelling place.

JENNY: I dinna ken.

COMMISSIONER: **(quietly menacing)** Oh, I think you ken mair than your sayin Jennifer Mathie. Satan has powers that canna be explainit . . . especially when he has the help o' a willing accomplice.

GAOLER: Sir, if I may be so bold to suggest.

COMMISSIONER: Yes, Henry you have another little device for loosening lockit tongues?

GAOLER: I have many Sir, but this one's stubborn. I ken the type. But her daughter's here. Her marrit daughter fae Glasgow. Perhaps we micht enlist her aid in this matter.

COMMISSIONER: Why not Henry? Show her in.

GAOLER unlocks door and calls.

GAOLER: Mary Robertson . . . you can come through now.

MARY enters followed by another minister.

GAOLER: Jist a minute mannie. Whaur did ye spring fae?

COMMISSIONER: It's all richt Henry. Weel, weel, the Reverend Mr Bell . . . if I'm not mistaken. To what do we owe this dubious honour.

MARY: I askit him to come hear. He kens your weys. **(Tearfully.)** Whit hae you done to my mither?

COMMISSIONER: Nothing yet my dear. We're merely trying to find the truth o' this unfortunate affair. Look, see for yourself! Your mother is as obstinate as ever.

MARY crosses to her.

MARY: Mother, Mother it's me! Open your eyes Mother! It's Mary. Tell me you're aw richt.

REVD. BELL: She's exhaustit Mary. They hae deprivit her o' sleep. It's yin o' their ploys.

COMMISSIONER: D'ye hear that Mr. Reid? The Reverent Bell thinks he's something of an expert in our ways.

REVD. REID: I am familiar wi his publication. He's a disgrace to the cloth!

COMMISSIONER: More than that Mr Reid . . . he's a danger to his flock. Anyone who defends witches seems to me to be hand in hand wi Satan.

REVD. BELL **(angrily)** If you'd read my treatise properly you'd be aware that I speak out only against injustice. You ken how much harm has been done to worthy and innocent people like Jenny Mathie here. You ken that old age, poverty, ill-looks and groundless fears are enough for some folk to defame their neighbours to the unspeakable prejudice of Christian charity. I've known Jenny Mathie for years. I admit she's made some enemies by the sharpness o' her tongue but she'd no more consort wi' Satan than I would.

JENNY: **(faintly)** Listen to him. He speaks the truth.

COMMISSIONER: **(smoothly menacing)** You're no preaching at your Conventicles now Mr Bell. You'll find I'm made of less gullible mettle. **(As REVEREND BELL starts at the mention of 'conventicles'.)** Did I startle you there Reverend? I hope I didnae frighten you . . . **(Crosses to him.)** You surely realise, do you not, that it's only a matter o' time before you Covenanters are roundit up. Next time you're preachin' oot there in the fields you had better keep glancin' ower your shoulder.

REVD. BELL: If you think you're going to silence me with your veiled threats then you're wrong. They'll hae to rip out ma tongue afore I stop speakin' against the burnin' o innocent people and the torturin o' poor folk of more goodness and esteem than most of their calumniators.

COMMISSIONER: Dinna give me your self–righteous indignation, Reverend. I'm merely doin' my job.

REVD. BELL: I believe Pontius Pilate offert the same excuse.

REVD. REID: How dare you liken the trial of Jesus Christ to that of this witch! You blaspheme! I shall pray for your soul.

REVD. BELL: Save your prayers for poor Jenny here. That she has the strength to resist all false accusation, and that you remember your Christian duty and ensure she has a fair trial.

MARY: **(tearfully)** Don't give in to them Mother. Pray for strength.

JENNY: They've makit up their minds Mary, but they'll no hear false testimony fae my lips. Dinna you fash. I've had three score year. It's been mair than enough.

MARY: Dinna talk like that Mother.

JENNY: Dinna greet. I'm a cheugh auld bird. **(Manages a smile.)** An' I'm nae deid yet.

COMMISSIONER: Perhaps you would be good enough to show them out. Henry, we have God's work to do.

REVD. REID: If I may pass on one word of advice from the Apostle Peter, Chapter I, verse eight, 'Be sober, be vigilant because your adversary the devil, as a roaring lion walketh about seeking whom he may devour'.

MARY and REVEREND BELL look at him in disbelief and are ushered out by the gaoler.

Scene 7

The drawing room at Pollok House.

GILBERT PETTIGREW sings to the assembled company. He is MARGARET's current beau. Watching him are SIR GEORGE MAXWELL, his daughter MARGARET, and three guests,

DOCTOR BREMNER, GEORGE SINCLAIR, Professor of Philosophy at Glasgow University and his wife. She is a twittering bird of a woman.

GILBERT finishes his song to polite applause.

SIR GEORGE: That was grand! You're in fine voice tonight, Gilbert.

MRS. SINCLAIR: **(twittering)** Oh it was beautiful! So moving!

GILBERT: Thank you, Maam.

SIR GEORGE: Aye . . . I see now . . . you've sung your way intil ma daughter's affections.

MARGARET: **(embarrassed)** Father! If I wasna sae pleased to see you up and aboot I'd be richt angry wi you!

MRS. SINCLAIR: Its so guid to see you restorit, Sir George . . . I was beside masel wi worry. Wasn't I my love?

PROF. SINCLAIR: Aye, we were both concernit, but as I telt my wife, Sir George, you've an iron constitution. If anyone can fight affliction you can.

SIR GEORGE: Weel, I had the best o'care from Doctor Bremner here. Twas his skill that pullt me through.

DR. BREMNER: It was none of my doing, Sir George. If you've any yin to thank, it's that lass Janet Douglas.

SIR GEORGE: I'm no sae sure o' that.

MARGARET: **(indignant)** How can you say that, faither? You were at death's door till she found the cause.

SIR GEORGE: I'm no so convincit as you, Meg. It might hae been sheer coincidence . . . like the restorin' o' her speech at the moment o' my recovery. **(Cynically.)** Now there's a mystery for ye.

MRS SINCLAIR: I'm confusit here. I thocht they'd found the yin who bewitchit you.

MARGARET: They have Mistress Sinclair, but father here is aye stubborn. He refuses to believe that evil woman is a witch.

SIR GEORGE: **(patiently)** I hae kent Jenny Mathie for nigh on thirty year. If she was a witch we'd hae seen evidence o' it afore now.

PROF. SINCLAIR: Have you expressit these doubts to the Commissioner for Witchcraft?

SIR GEORGE: I tried . . . but yon mannie sees only siller signs. He's linit his pockets frae his confessit witches. He'll no let poor Jenny Mathie slip oot his grasp so easy.

MARGARET: I canna understand you, father. You ken how ill you were. If it wasna for Janet you wouldna be here to debate the matter.

SIR GEORGE: I prefer to think the Guid Lord had a hand in it.

PROF. SINCLAIR: Maybe He did. Perhaps this Janet Douglas was His instrument.

GILBERT: You think that's possible, sir?

MRS. SINCLAIR: There are many references in Holy Scripture to white witches, Mr. Pettigrew . . . maybe this lass is one of them.

PROF. SINCLAIR: **(hastily)** Let us not jump to conclusions ower quickly. I'd like to do as we discussit, Sir George and talk to this young lady. . . . She's here in your employ now I believe?

SIR GEORGE: Aye . . . this week past. It was Meg's idea . . . none of my doing.

MARGARET **(reprovingly)** Twas the least we could do. Provide her with a roof ower her head.

SIR GEORGE: Perhaps Meg you would be good enough to take our guests to the gallery to view our new purchases.

MRS. SINCLAIR: Oh, I'm longing to see your new paintings . . . from the Dutch School I believe, Sir George. I try to persuade my husband that works of art are necessary for every civilised household, but I fear he is a Philistine in such matters.

PROF. SINCLAIR: I have more practical needs for my siller, my dear. Keeping you in fine dresses is only one of them.

MRS. SINCLAIR: Oh, listen to him. Anyone would think I was extravagant.

MARGARET: If you would come this way, Mrs. Sinclair.

SIR GEORGE: Meg . . . would you send Janet Douglas to me. I am most grateful for your visit, Professor. This wretchit business has wrackit my mind as weel as my body.

PROF. SINCLAIR: I gathered from whit you said earlier that you were troubled. Tell me whit ails you . . . what you really think o' this affair.

SIR GEORGE: I dinna ken whit to think . . . wi aw this talk o' witchcraft and noo the incarceration o' the widow Stewart . . . I feel somewhit responsible.

PROF. SINCLAIR: Now ye're no tellin' me Sir George that a man who's come as far as you have in society, suffers yet fae oor national affliction.

SIR GEORGE: To which particular affliction do you refer, Professor? We hae so many.

PROF. SINCLAIR: Yin of self-doubt. The habit o' beating oorsels on the breist in moments o' crisis or when things seem beyond oor ken.

SIR GEORGE: Aye . . . weel I fear I must plead guilty to that charge, but then I find the disposition of those who flail awa at folk unable to defend themselves even mair reprehensible. Seems to me those pernicious wretches tend to find their targets in the weakest and most vulnerable breists.

PROF. SINCLAIR: But that tendency is, regrettably, a universal one.

SIR GEORGE: Maybe so . . . but roon here we hae an unnatural appetite for it.

PROF. SINCLAIR: Have you considert that those self-same appetites may look for satisfaction in unusual places.

SIR GEORGE: I'm not sure I understand you, Professor.

PROF. SINCLAIR: I'm suggesting that there are those amang us who find the canons of law and church do nothing but keep them in their place. If that place is not pleasing to them then they might be inclinit to invoke other help and **(shrugs)** to Hell with the consequence, **(smiles grimly)** literally.

SIR GEORGE: You mean the help of Satan? You think that there may be truth in Janet Douglas' story. That the widow Stewart practised his evil rites.

PROF. SINCLAIR: Anything is possible Sir George. I merely suggest we keep our minds open to any circumstance.

SIR GEORGE: **(troubled)** Of course.

PROF. SINCLAIR: You have told Janet Douglas of my visit?

SIR GEORGE: No, I thought it best to catch her unpreparit.

PROF. SINCLAIR: You think she is a scheming lass, then?

SIR GEORGE: **(disturbed)** No . . . it's not that. I honestly dinna ken what to make of her. I've no encountert her like afore. You see she . . .

JANET glides in silently behind them. SIR GEORGE turns round surprised.

SIR GEORGE: Oh . . . I didna hear you come in, lass. Janet, this is Professor Sinclair of Glasgow University. He is Professor of Philosophy there. He wants very much to meet you.

SINCLAIR holds out his hand to shake JANET's.

PROF. SINCLAIR: I'm delighted to make your acquaintance Janet. I've heard a lot about you.

She says nothing. Just looks at him inscrutably, quite cool and composed.

PROF. SINCLAIR: Sir George has telt you the nature o' my subject. Do you know what philosophy is, Janet?

JANET: The seeking after wisdom or knowledge, sir. In particular, that which deals with ultimate reality.

SINCLAIR and SIR GEORGE exchange surprised looks.

PROF. SINCLAIR: Correct, Janet. I seek knowledge. I wish to know more about you, my dear. Sir George has telt me something of your powers. I would like to ask you some questions about yourself. Have you no objection?

JANET: I do not like answering questions, sir. It pains me.

SINCLAIR takes a silver coin from his pocket and hands it to her.

PROF. SINCLAIR: I have found that silver has pain reducing qualities. What say you?

JANET: **(smoothly)** I will answer where I can, sir.

PROF. SINCLAIR: Good . . . I understand that when Lady Margaret met you at the Glasgow Fair you appeared to have lost the power of speech. Was this a fairground trick or a genuine affliction?

JANET: It was no trick sir. I was without speech.

PROF. SINCLAIR. For how long had you suffered this loss?

JANET: For as long as I can remember.

PROF. SINCLAIR: **(musingly)** Yet you speak as one practised in language. How do you account for that?

JANET: I cannot, sir.

PROF. SINCLAIR: Can you account for your recovery?

JANET: It was the embrocation.

SIR GEORGE: **(surprised)** Embrocation?

JANET: Yes, Sir George . . . *Album Graecum*, I applied it every night as revealit.

SIR GEORGE: Revealit?

JANET: In my vision sir. I was told to apply it every night around the throat.

PROF. SINCLAIR Have you any of this miraculous mixture left?

JANET: No sir. I was using the last of it when my speech returnit.

PROF. SINCLAIR: I see . . . and the container?

JANET: Thrown away. I had no further use of it.

PROFESSOR SINCLAIR opens his bag and extracts two books. he hands one to JANET. An English translation of Sophocles *Electra*.

PROF. SINCLAIR: Would you open that book and read from it. Any page you like.

JANET opens it and without hesitation reads Electra's speech.

JANET: 'Brother in Heaven's name
Let him not speak a word or plead his cause.
When a poor wretch is in the toils of fate
What can a brief reprieve avail him? No slay him
outright and having slain him give his corpse
to such grave makers as is meet,
far from our sight.'

The PROFESSOR and SIR GEORGE exchange surprised looks.

PROF. SINCLAIR: You are familiar with the writing of Sophocles?

JANET: No, sir.

PROF. SINCLAIR: You read very fluently. **(He hands her another book. This time is Euripedes *The Bacchae* in Greek.)** Try this one if you will.

She opens it at the last page and reads without hesitation.

JANET: 'There be many shapes of mystery
And many things God makes to be,
Past hopes or fear.
And the end men looketh for cometh not,
And a path is there where no man thought
So hath it fallen here.'

PROF. SINCLAIR: Why did you choose that particular passage from Euripides.

JANET: **(shrugs)** Because I liked it.

PROF. SINCLAIR: Are you aware that you were translating it from Greek?

JANET: No, sir.

SIR GEORGE: Where did you learn to speak Greek?

JANET: I don't know sir.

SIR GEORGE: **(frustrated)** Come, come lass. You must ken where you were schoolit!

PROF. SINCLAIR holds up a restraining hand.

PROF. SINCLAIR: Sit down, lass. Perhaps you would care for a glass of something. I'm sure Sir George has no objection,

JANET: **(sits)** I want nothing sir. Thank you.

PROF. SINCLAIR: Janet Douglas . . . that is your given name?

JANET: It was the name I was called by all who knew me.

PROF. SINCLAIR: Who are your parents?

JANET: I don't remember, sir.

SIR GEORGE: **(impatiently)** Someone must have brought you up.

JANET: **(looking a little upset)** Yes.

PROF. SINCLAIR: **(gently)** Who was it Janet?

JANET: I was kept when I was very young by a poor woman.

PROF. SINCLAIR: Was she a relative?

JANET: No sir.

PROF. SINCLAIR: How did you come to be there?

JANET: I don't know sir.

SIR GEORGE: Is this woman . . . still alive?

JANET: She may be sir.

SIR GEORGE: You don't keep in touch with the woman who brought you up. That seems a little ungrateful.

JANET: She was cruel to me, sir.

PROF SINCLAIR: In what way?

JANET: Beat me, starved me. That's why I ran away.

PROF. SINCLAIR: I see. . . . You must have hated her?

JANET: We were very poor. She had little enough for herself. So she let others abuse me for payment.

PROF. SINCLAIR: **(exchanging a look with SIR GEORGE)** I see. . . . Have you any knowledge of religion, Janet?

JANET: None sir. I am ignorant of its principles . . . though I know the Lord's prayer slightly.

PROF. SINCLAIR: Where did you learn that?

JANET: I didn't sir but I heard the witches repeat it in my dream . . . then they changed the words to make it honour Satan.

PROF. SINCLAIR: Do you communicate with the Devil or any other spirit?

JANET: No sir. But the Devil is represented to me when I see the evil work of witches. I see him in the shape and habit as they do.

PROF. SINCLAIR: If we may turn to the business of Sir George's illness. How did you know that Jennifer Mathie had bewitchit Sir George here?

JANET: I saw it, sir.

PROF. SINCLAIR: How do you mean?

JANET: In a vision.

PROF. SINCLAIR: What exactly did you see in this vision?

JANET: **(becoming slightly agitated)** I saw Jennifer Mathie make a waxen image in which she stuck pins. I saw her calling on the devil to punish Sir George. I saw her hiding the likeness o' Sir George behind the fireplace.

PROF. SINCLAIR: It's all richt lass. Nae need to be feart. The perpetrator is ahint bars. She cannot harm you.

JANET: **(increasingly disturbed)** There are others who follow in her wake. They invoke the crooked serpent. They walk hand in hand with Satan. They will carry out his will. They must be stopped. They must be stopped! **(She lets out a cry.)** I see him.

Lights go up on an upper level. We see JOHN STEWART silhouetted. He holds a clay image of a man in his hand.

PROF. SINCLAIR: Who do you see Janet? What do you see?

As JANET speaks SIR GEORGE clutches at his throat, fighting for breath.

JANET: I see the son of Janet Mathie. He is in league with the evil one, the Prince of Darkness. He has a clay image of a man in his hand. Oh, no . . . stop him. Stop him. No, no . . . you musn't. **(Screams.)** He's casting it into the fire! *Aagh*!

We see a sheet of flame rise beside JOHN STEWART.

SIR GEORGE lets out a terrible cry and falls motionless to the ground. PROFESSOR SINCLAIR rushes over to him. JANET stares fixedly ahead.

PROF. SINCLAIR: **(bending over SIR GEORGE)** Sir George . . . speak to me man. For the Lords sake say something. **(He feels for a pulse.)** Oh, my God . . . there's no pulse . . . **(To JANET.)** Do something woman . . . for pity's sake . . . get Dr. Bremner!

JANET still remains staring fixedly ahead.

PROF. SINCLAIR: **(calling)** Help . . . help Dr. Bremner, Margaret! Come quick please, please!

Fade.

Act 2

Scene 1

In the home of JOHN STEWART.

He is seated at a rough table drinking a jug of ale. By the look of him it is not his first. His sister ANNABIL scurries about making his meal. There is a bed in the corner.

JOHN: Hurry up . . . I'm stervin!

ANNABIL: I'm goin' as fast as I can, John.

JOHN: Weel it's no' fast enough. If I've to wait much longer you'll ken a' aboot it! A man works his airse aff a' day an' he expects a meal waitin' for him. If ony lad's daft enough to wed you then you'll hae to sharpen your ideas. Whit hae you been dain aw day?

ANNABIL: I went ower to oor ain hoose tae gie it a bit dicht. I want it to be shinin' for mother comin' oot the jail.

JOHN: If the talks to be beleivit . . . she'll no be comin' oot.

ANNABIL: **(distressed)** Whit hae you heard, John? Tell me!

JOHN: Weel they say . . . yon Commissioner for Witchcraft aye gets a conviction.

ANNABIL: But Mother's done nothing. There's some aroon here dabble in that sort o' thing . . . but no Mother.

JOHN: **(jumps up)** Whit sort o' thing are you talkin' aboot?

ANNABIL: **(frightened)** Nothin'.

JOHN: **(grabbing her)** Just you keep your mooth shut, you hear. That kinna talk is dangerous.

ANNABIL: I've said nothin to naebody.

JOHN: Weel make sure you keep it that wey.

She moves away from him puts his meal in a bowl and gives it to him.

JOHN: Aboot time too. **(He takes a mouthful.)** No' bad . . . no bad'. You bide wi' me much longer, sister an' we'll mak a proper cook o' ye.

ANNABIL: **(fearfully)** John, what did you mean about the Commissioner aye getting a conviction. Mother will never confess. She's done nothing.

JOHN: Then they'll duck her in the river till she droons.

ANNABIL: **(distressed)** They canna dae that to an innocent person.

JOHN: Oh, they'll declare her innocent after she droons. That's their wey. If she floats she's a witch an' they burn her. If she sinks she's innocent. Fat lot o' good it'll dae her wi her lungs fu' o' watter.

There is a loud knocking on the door.

JOHN: **(alarmed)** Who the hell is that?

ANNABIL: **(running off)** Maybe its Mother. Maybe they've let her oot.

There is the sound of raised voices offstage. ANNABIL rushes back in.

ANNABIL: **(terrified)** John . . . John it's them . . .

The COMMISSIONER for Witchcraft enters. He is accompanied by two men armed with pikes. JANET DOUGLAS is with them.

JOHN: **(rising)** Whit's goin' on? Who the hell are you?

COMMISSIONER: I'll ask the questions here.

He gesticulates and the two armed men stand either side of JOHN. Pikes pointed in his direction. ANNABIL cowers petrified.

COMMISSIONER: You are John Stewart son of Jennifer Mathie Stewart?

JOHN: **(defiant)** Aye . . . who wants to know?

The COMMISSIONER for Witchcraft nods to one of the armed men who hits JOHN in the ribs. He doubles over in pain.

COMMISSIONER: I don't think you're listening, Mister Stewart. **(He turns to ANNABIL.)** You are Annabil Stewart, sister of this stubborn fellow?

ANNABIL: **(terrified)** Y . . . yes, sir.

COMMISSIONER: How old are you Annabil?

ANNABIL: Fourteen, sir.

COMMISSIONER: You see, Mr Stewart . . . how polite . . . how co-operative your sister is. That's what I want from you. Now you asked who I was and . . . although you did not ask it ower nicely . . . I'll tell you. The name is Thomas Ramsay, Commissioner for Witchcraft.

ANNABIL gasps in fear.

COMMISSIONER: Why so feart m'dear? Surely you have nothing to hide. Have you?

ANNABIL: N . . . no no sir.

COMMISSIONER: **(closing in on her)** Yet it is my experience that if one member of a family practises that evil diabolic art which I am pledgit to destroy, then others of that breed may be similarly persuadit.

ANNABIL: No no . . . not me sir.

He spins round to face JOHN.

COMMISSIONER: And what about you Stewart? Although your Mother has no yet confessit we hae enough evidence to burn her for witchcraft.

ANNABIL gasps.

COMMISSIONER: Now what tricks did you learn at your mother's knee, John eh?

JOHN: I dinna ken what you're talking about.

COMMISSIONER: Now now John dinna blacken your soul ony mair. The talk in the Shaws is . . . you're a warlock!

JOHN: That's nonsense. I'm nae mair guilty than my mother!

COMMISSIONER: Oh, that's a poor defence John. If we have to save you from the same fate as will befallit your mother . . . then we best check oot your story. I take it you have nae objection if we search your premises.

JOHN: Go ahead. I've nothin' to hide.

COMMISSIONER: Oh, isn't that touching. I do believe your mother usit the self same words.

He gestures to the two armed men who start turning the place over. JANET watches then crosses to the COMMISSIONER and points to the bed.

ANNABIL: **(almost a whisper)** Oh . . . no . . . I hae nothing to do with it.

COMISSIONER: John Stewart . . . come ower here and light a candle.

JOHN takes his tinder box (flint steel and scorched rags) and with a sulphur match lights a candle.

COMMISSIONER: Now if we find onything here as Janet Douglas has foreseen, I want nae talk o' collusion. Janet awa and stand in the far corner ower there. Annabil, you go with her. Now I call on you men, James Dunlop and Ludowick Frazer of Househill to witness that Janet Douglas is far removit from this bed What say ye?

JAMES/LUDOWICK: Aye sir.

COMMISSIONER: Come nearer John Stewart. **(Nods to his men.)** Right . . . you may proceed.

They pull back the bedclothes and start looking amongst the bedstraw. LUDOWICK lifts the bolster and lifts out a clay effigy partly concealed in the straw.

LUDOWICK: **(triumphantly)** Here we are Commissioner.

COMMISSIONER: Bring it ower!

LUDOWICK: **(handing it over)** Be careful sir! Tis fresh made and liable to break.

COMMISSIONER: Well, well, look here gentlemen. Witness this. James what do you see?

JAMES: A clay likenes sir?

COMMISSIONER: What else do you see Ludowick?

LUDOWICK: Three pins in the figure, sir.

COMMISSIONER: Where be they placed?

LUDOWICK: Two in the side and one in the breest.

COMMISSIONER: You hear that Stewart, before two independent witnesses. What have you to say for yourself?

JOHN says nothing.

COMMISSIONER: Come come Mr Stewart. Are we to take it that your silence is an admission of guilt?

JOHN: Somebody pit it there.

COMMISSIONER: Now, now, Mr Stewart, you can do better than that. Your own mother yased that yin.

JOHN: I ken nothin' aboot it

COMMISSIONER: Oh, I think a wee spell in the prison hoose o' Paisley may loosen your tongue. **(Formal.)** John Stewart of Pollokshaws, on the authority of the Earl Of Dundonald and Lord Ross of His Majesty's Privy Council I herefore arrest you for the crime of sorcery. **(He turns to ANNABIL.)** Annabil Stewart . . . have you anything to say of your part in this matter?

ANNABIL: I ken nothing.

COMMISSIONER: Yet you seemed to ken there was something under that bolster?

ANNABIL starts to cry.

COMMISSIONER: I hae seen ower mony witches tears to be movit. Take them away.

JOHN and ANNABIL are marched off at pike-point.

COMMISSIONER: Miss Douglas it appears His Majesty's Privy Council is indebtit to you.

He follows them out.

JANET DOUGLAS is left alone onstage. She gives a strange little half-smile.

Slow Fade.

Scene 2

Anteroom at Pollok Castle. LAURENCE ushers in MARY ROBERTSON.

LAURENCE: Mary Robertson, Sir George.

LAURENCE stands in watchful attendance.

SIR GEORGE: Thank you Laurence. You may leave us.

LAURENCE: **(protesting)** But Sir George . . .

SIR GEORGE: **(firmly)** Laurence!

LAURENCE: **(for MARY's benefit)** I'll be outside the door if you need me, sir.

SIR GEORGE: My servants seem to think I have something to fear from you Mistress Robertson. Is that so?

MARY: No, indeed . . . I swear not sir . . . You ken who I am?

SIR GEORGE: The daughter of Jenny Mathie Stewart, and sister to Annabil and John . . . at present in custody for attemptit injury to my person, through paction wi' the devil.

MARY: **(earnestly)** It's not true Sir. My family hae nothing agin you.

SIR GEORGE: My household is of a different opinion. They urged me not to see you. I feel however, if you've come all the way from Glasgow you may be able to throw some light on this wretchit business.

MARY: **(agitated)** I've been waiting for twa days to see you. The river was so swelt up I couldna get across to your hoose afore now. Sir, my family are innocent. I want you to intercede on their behalf.

SIR GEORGE: **(taken aback)** You ken, do you not, that I was at deaths door until your family was arrestit. I am the last person you should ask.

MARY: But you kent my mother and father for many years. They spent a lifetime in your employ and served you faithfully. You must know this is none of my mother's doing.

SIR GEORGE: But what of your brother John?

MARY: My brother is a fool sir, but he's nae warlock.

SIR GEORGE: It appears your sister Annabil is of a different opinion.

MARY: **(fearfully)** Whit do you mean?

SIR GEORGE: I mean that she has now confessit.

MARY: To what?

SIR GEORGE: A paction with others to invoke the Devil's malice agin the family of Pollok.

MARY: It's not true . . . What others? Who else did she name?

SIR GEORGE: Your mother, brother and several neighbours who bide on my estate . . . Bessie Weir, Margery Craige and Margaret Jackson.

MARY: I canny believe this.

SIR GEORGE: I must confess I found it difficult to grasp myself.

But when the Depute Sheriff o' Renfrew himself found the insensible marks on their person, I had to be convincit.

MARY: Insensible marks . . . you mean witches marks?

SIR GEORGE: Aye lass . . . your mother was covert in them. She still insists she's innocent but when they found them on your brother he broke doon and confessit.

MARY: **(tearfully)** It canna be.

SIR GEORGE: There, there lass, I understand your feelings but maybe you should just be thankin' the guid Lord that you were merrit and awa fae your family or you too might hae been taintit.

MARY: But it's not true I tell you. It's her doing.

SIR GEORGE: Who?

MARY: Janet Douglas . . . she's responsible!

SIR GEORGE: Whit do you know of Janet Douglas?

MARY: I met her at the Glesca Fair. She has strange powers. I took her in when she had naewhere to go. Why is she dain this to my family? They've done nothing to her.

SIR GEORGE: **(thoughtfully)** So you think she is behind this?

MARY: I know she is? But I canna understand why.

SIR GEORGE: Well, perhaps you should put that question to her yoursel.

He walks to the door and calls 'Laurence'.

LAURENCE: Yes sir . . . I'm here. Is everything a richt?

SIR GEORGE: Of course it is. This lady doesna bite. Ask Janet Douglas to come here will you. **(He turns back to MARY.)** Whatever your fears are on this matter let me assure you your faimily will get a fair trial.

MARY: The Reverend Bell says naebody gets acquitit when they're accused of witchcraft.

SIR GEORGE: Although I hae great sympathy wi' the Reverend Bell and the Covenanting cause he's no entirely blameless on that score. Seems to me his fellow clergymen hae been first to the taper when witches were tried. They seem to see sorcery aw aroon them.

MARY: He's not like that.

SIR GEORGE: So I believe, and neither are the men who will be trying your family and the other poor wretches. We hae some of the finest members of the judiciary in the land .Sir Patrick Gauston, James Brisbane of Bishopton, Sir John Shaw of Greenock and John Preston the Advocate. They have appointit Lord Ross as Judge Assessor with power to vote and decide. These men will no' be easily swayt. You can be assurit . . . **(He breaks of as JANET DOUGLAS appears.)** Ah . . . Janet . . . I believe you ken Mistress Robertson.

JANET looks cooly at MARY but says nothing.

MARY: Why are you doing this to my faimily? What harm have they done you?

JANET: They are guilty of witchcraft.

MARY: That's not true and you ken it.

SIR GEORGE: Janet . . . how do you come to this knowledge of witchcraft?

MARY: Because she's one hersel' that's how?

SIR GEORGE holds up a restraining hand.

SIR GEORGE: How did you know about these likenesses made of me that brought me down so terribly.

JANET: I saw it in a vision sir. It was revealit to me.

SIR GEORGE: How can this be?

JANET: I dont know sir. I know these things as if I were present at their happening. I saw the coven wi Jennifer Mathie and her son present. They consort wi the evil one. They must be punishit!

MARY: **(angry)** You liar . . .

She rushes towards her. JANET lets out a terrible eerie cry and puts out her hand to stop her.

JANET: Do not touch me Daughter of Beelzebub . . . you are one of them! **(JANET holds her head in a trance like state.)** I can see . . . You have consorted with the evil serpent. You lie with the Prince of Darkness. Sister of Satan confess and repent for your end is nigh. You will plunge into the dark waters with your blackened soul. Confess and repent before its too late.

SIR GEORGE who has been transfixed during this scene moves towards her.

SIR GEORGE: What are you saying?

JANET: **(pointing her finger accusingly)** I say Mary Robertson that you are a witch!!

MARY: **(distressed)** That's not true. Sir George dinna believe her. She speaks falsely.

JANET moves across to MARY and with great force rips the collar from her dress.

JANET: See! She has the insensible mark. Do you deny now Mary Robertson the proof before your eyes? The mark which Satan put upon you . . . the mark of a witch?

MARY lets out a long piercing scream and runs off. SIR GEORGE stands stunned. JANET stands looking inscrutable.

Fade.

A piece of solemn and dramatic music is played before the next scene.

Scene 3

As the music is being played the next scene is set up.

February 15th 1667 The Justice Court, Paisley. The trial of the witches before the commissioners of the judiciary. On one side of the court sit the accused . . . JENNIFER MATHIE STEWART, JOHN STEWART, ANNABIL STEWART, MARGARET JACKSON, BESSIE WEIR and MARGERY CRAIGE. Seated near them is their defence council SIR PATRICK GAUSTON. ANNABIL STEWART is in the witness box. On the bench sits the presiding Judge, LORD ROSS. The CLERK OF THE COURT writes down all the proceedings. The advocate JOHN PRESTON questions LAURENCE MARTIN.

PRESTON: Mr Martin, would you tell the court, in your own words, what happened on your visit to the accused Janet Mathie's house in Polloktoun on the 3rd of November last.

LAURENCE: Well sir we . . . that is, James Dunlop and myself went along to Janet Mathie's house accompanit by Janet Douglas and demandit to search her dwelling.

PRESTON: Did you give a reason for your search?

LAURENCE: Not at first sir. We didnae want to pit her on guard.

GAUSTON: **(rising)** Objection. The witness is pre-supposing the accused had something to hide.

LORD ROSS: Sustainit. Witness will confine himself to the question. **(To CLERK OF THE COURT.)** You will strike Mr Martin's words from the record.

PRESTON: What did Mistress Mathie say to your request.

LAURENCE: She telt me where to go Sir.

PRESTON: I take it by this she did not mean Pollokshaws?

LAURENCE: No, sir I mean she swore.

PRESTON: What did you do then?

LAURENCE: We explainit that she was under suspicion for the bewitching of Sir George Maxwell and if she wantit to clear her name she should let us search her dwelling.

PRESTON: And she let you in?

LAURENCE: Yes sir. She said she had nothing to hide.

PRESTON: Please confine yourself to the question, Mr Martin.

LAURENCE: Sorry sir.

MR PRESTON: Would you tell us in your own words . . . what happened next.

LAURENCE: Well Sir, I stood beside Mistress Mathie while James . . . Mr Dunlop searchit ahint the fireplace. He then found a waxen figure with three pins placit in it which we took awa.

MR. PRESTON. Did you observe Janet Douglas during the finding of the waxen object?

LAURENCE: Aye sir?

MR PRESTON: Where was she in the room?

LAURENCE: She was near the fireplace, sir.

MR PRESTON: How near?

LAURENCE: Oh . . . aboot twa arm lengths distant.

MR PRESTON: I see. Would it have been possible for her to place anything behind the fireplace?

GAUSTON: Objection. This is conjecture

ROSS: Over ruled. Witness will answer the question.

LAURENCE: Nae withoot my observin it sir?

MR PRESTON: And did you see her place anything there?

LAURENCE: No sir. I watchit her and she didna move.

JENNY rises furious.

JENNY: She pit it there I tell you. She's the one wha should be on trial nae me.

LORD ROSS: You are no' helpin your case by showin disrespect to the court. If you interrupt the proceedings again I will hae you ejectit fae the room.

PRESTON: One final question. M'Lord. You told us earlier of the poor state of Sir George's health prior to your visit to Mistress Mathie. What was his state of health after you returnit and removit the pins from the effigy found there.

LAURENCE: It was miraculous Sir. The colour had returnit to his cheeks and he was like his old self again.

PRESTON: Thank you Mr Martin. No further questions.

LORD ROSS: You may step down, Mr Martin.

MARTIN joins the observers in the court.

CLERK: I call Annabil Stewart to the witness stand.

ANNABIL rises terrified. Her mother squeezes her hand. She withdraws hers hastily and avoids looking at her mother.

LORD ROSS: I would remind the witness that she is still on oath.

PRESTON: You are Annabil Stewart daughter of Jennifer Mathie Stewart?

ANNABIL: Yes, sir

PRESTON: Miss Stewart, I would like you to tell the court in your own words of the events which happened on Harvest last, when you returnit to your mother's house to find three of the accused here present.

ANNABIL: Well . . . sir. On Harvest last I came home from my work on Sir George Maxwell's estate to find Bessie Weir, Margery Craige and Margaret Jackson all present at my mother's house. I had been at home but five minutes when . . . when . . . the Devil appearit, and demandit that I give myself to him. I did not want to do this for I was feart. The Devil was all in black and he scarit me . . . My Mother said if I did as he requestit I would get a new coat and the Devil was very nice to me. Telt me to call him Ejoal and promisit me onythin' I wantit. Instructit by my mother and the other women present, I pit ma hand to the crown o' my head and the other to the sole of my foot and did give myself up to him. After that the Devil lay abed with me under the clothes. I wantit him to stay away for he was cold but he placed me nearest to him. When I awoke Bessie Weir was turning a waxen image on a spit before the fire. The Devil, Bessie Weir, Margery Craige, Margaret Jackson and my mother Jennifer Mathie all repeatit the name 'Sir George Maxwell' as she turnit.

The lights fade on ANNABIL and come up on JOHN STEWART.

JOHN: On Wednesday the third of January last I had just gone to bed when I heard someone call me by name. I awoke and saw a man there dressit in black wi' bluish hancuffs. He had hoggers on his legs and was without shoes. When he spoke his voice was hough and goustie and I kent him to be the Devil. I lit a candle and found that Bessie Weir, Margaret Jackson and Margery Craige had already enterit my house through the window. They said that they had invokit the Devil's help to avenge the taking of my mother Jennifer Mathie, who was at that time in the Paisley Jail. In return I should not want for any pleesure. After placing yin hand on my head and the other on the sole of my foot I was gien the spirit name Jonas. The Devil askit oor consent for the making of an effigy to tak away the life o Sir George Maxwell o' Pollok. The women wrought the clay and the Devil made the face hands and legs. I held the candle while he did this and saw by its light that his feet were cloven. While the Devil was placing three pins in the clay figure my sister Annabil came to the house and remainit during the proceedings.

Lights go down on him and up on MARGARET JACKSON.

MARGARET: I am Margaret Jackson relict of the late Thomas Jackson of Pollokshaws. Bessie Weir came to me for help in obtaining her revenge on Sir George Maxwell of Pollok. Sir George had refusit to enter her husband in his Harvest service and causit her bairns to hae little to live on as a consequence. Bessie kent that my acquaintance wi the devil went further back than hers. Some forty years ago he first came to me when I was at Pollokshaws-croft carrying a few sticks on my back. He offert to carry them for me and said he could lighten my load permanent-like if I gave myself to him. I renouncit my baptism and was given the name Locas. On the third of January last I woke up and found a man in my bed. I thought at first it was my husband but he's been dead twenty years or therebye. I kent then it was the Devil and he telt me to form a paction wi' Jennifer Mathie Stewart and her family together with Bessie Weir and Margery Craige . . . the purpose o' which was to bring aboot the daith o' Sir George Maxwell o' Pollok. We met and agreeit to this.

We hear a cry. The lights go on suddenly.

JENNIFER MATHIE is on her feet.

JENNY: It's aw lies. I ken nothin' o this. They've been forcit to say this. It's not true.

LORD ROSS: Mistress Mathie I have already warnit you about interrupting court proceedings. I have no alternative but to ban you from the court herewith. Take her away.

A man armed with a pike leads her away shouting.

JENNIFER: It's Janet Douglas' doing. She's the yin you should be trying. She's foolt the lot o' ye!

LORD ROSS: Milords of the Privy Council you have heard the evidence before you and the confessions of John Stewart, Annabil Stewart, Margery Craige, Bessie Weir and Margaret Jackson to the bewitching of Sir George Maxwell of Pollok. Only Jennifer Mathie Stewart remains stubborn in her obstinancy. However we have heard evidence from her gaoler at Paisley prison who swore on oath that though Mathie's feet were fixit in the stocks, she had movit those stocks six yards in order to obtain a bolster for her head. Bear in mind that two of the strongest men in the country could barely lift them, and consider, if you need, that this is further evidence of her sorcery. She has by reputation been branded a witch for some years, although this is often the case with innocent people of mature years. However, conclusive proof, if such you require, is the finding of many insensible marks . . . commonly known as witches marks upon her person.

During this speech the lights have dimmed on the rest of the stage focussing on LORD ROSS only. As he mentions the accused names lights come up on them.

LORD ROSS: I therefore find Jennifer Mathie Stewart

(We see her tied to a stake.)

John Stewart,

(We see him similarly tied.)

Bessie Weir,

(Tied to stake.)

Margaret Jackson,

(Tied to stake.)

Margerey Craige,

(Tied to stake.)

and Annabil Stewart, all guilty of witchcraft.

ANNABIL STEWART (lights on her).

LORD ROSS: In view of your youth and penitency it has been decidit by the Lords of the Council that your life will be sparit. However you will remain in the Prison House of Paisley for ten years. However youthful ignorance cannot be pleadit for the rest of you. In attempting to take away the life of another by sorcery, you deserve the severest penalty this court can award. On Monday next therefore, the fourth of February, in the year of our Lord sixteen hundred and sixty seven Jennifer Mathie Stewart, John Stewart, Bessie Weir, Margery Craig and Margaret Jackson . . . **(The fires are lit (dry ice and red lighting etc).)** you will be condemmit to the fire to be burned and your effigies with you. May the Lord have mercy on your souls.

The conflagration builds. The five figures barely distinguishable through the flames.

Blackout.

Sombre music is played before scene four.

Scene 4

Glasgow at the home of Rob and Mary Robertson. ROB sits head in hands, alone on stage. There is a thunderous knocking on the door.

ROB: **(calls wearily)** It's nae lockit.

The COMMISSIONER for Witchcraft enters accompanied by SIR GEORGE MAXWELL and a man armed with a pike.

ROB stands startled as he sees them.

ROB: Whit the? . . .

COMMISSIONER: Robert Robertson?

ROB: Aye . . . whits a' this?

COMMISSIONER: You are husband to Mary Robertson, sweetmeat seller and daughter of the late Jennifer Mathie Stewart?

ROB: Aye.

COMMISSIONER: I have a warrant here signed by Lord Ross and co-signed by the Magistrates o' Glasgow for the arrest of Mary Robertson for the crime o' witchcraft.

ROB: **(bitterly)** You're too late.

COMMISSIONER: You mean the bird has flown. We'll see about that. **(To armed man.)** Search the place!

As the man starts to move.

ROB: I mean she's nae longer wi' us.

COMMISSIONER: Where is she Robertson? Come on . . . we'll find her anyway.

ROB: Then you'll need to go to the bottom o' the river.

SIR GEORGE: **(startled)** What are you saying man?

ROB: **(breaking down)** I'm saying my Mary . . . ma lovely lass, droont hersel' in the Clyde on Tuesday last.

COMMISSIONER: You mean she committed suicide?

ROB: **(angry)** No! She widnae dae that. My Mary loved life ower much for that.

SIR GEORGE: **(almost to himself)** She foretelt this.

ROB: She did it to her! That Janet Douglas! We gave her food, shelter. Why has she done this to us? **(Sobs.)** My Mary . . . my lovely Mary . . .

SIR GEORGE: Janet Douglas . . . that name again.

COMMISSIONER: Can you throw some light on this, Sir George?

SIR GEORGE: Aye Commissioner . . . as you know Janet was in my employ til fower weeks ago when she up and left. Mary Robertson came to my house and accusit her of givin' false testimony agin her family . . .

COMMISSIONER: **(impatiently)** Aye . . . aye I'm aware o' aw this Sir George but . . .

SIR GEORGE: I telt you she found the witch's mark on Mary Robertson.

COMMISSIONER: **(even more impatient)** Yes sir, I ken . . . that's why we're here.

SIR GEORGE: But Janet Douglas foretelt her death. She telt Mary Robertson she would 'plunge into the dark waters.'

ROB: **(angry)** The bitch! The whore! She's the yin responsible for aw this. She put the fear o' death into my Mary. My lass widnae hae hermed a fly. She was aye dain kindnesses to fowk. That Janet Douglas turnt her mind . . . made her think Satan had pit his merk on her. It was lies . . . aw lies.

COMMISSIONER: **(smoothly)** Perhaps not, Mr Robertson. After all her whole family seemed to have mair than dabbled in sorcery. What makes you think your wife was any different?

ROB: **(grabbing him by the throat)** Because I wis merrit to her for twinty-two years ya swine! Thats why!

The armed man and SIR GEORGE pull ROB off.

SIR GEORGE: Calm down Mr. Robertson. The Commissioner is merely trying to get at the truth.

ROB: Then you should be doon at the Candleworks questioning her.

COMMISSIONER: **(rubbing his throat)** Janet Douglas is at the Candleworks? Here in Glasgow?

ROB: **(bitterly)** Aye she's only been there but a few weeks and already she's causit trouble.

SIR GEORGE: What kind of trouble Mr Robertson?

ROB: She accusit yin o' the workers there . . . an auld wifie that never did ony herm to naebody o' bein a witch. From whit they say, the poor auld sowel has lost her wits . . . disnae ken her ain kin ony mair.

The COMMISSIONER and SIR GEORGE exchange looks.

ROB: **(earnestly)** For the love o' God stop her sir, before she causes any mair trouble! I dinna ken why she's dain this but she must be stoppit!

COMMISSIONER: Yes perhaps it is time I paid another visit to Miss Douglas. **(To armed man.)** Come with me!

COMMISIONER and armed man hurry out. SIR GEORGE goes to follow them, then turns back to ROB.

SIR GEORGE: You hae my sympathy in your sad loss, sir . . . and my prayers. May the Lord bring you comfort, this day.

He leaves. ROB is left, head in hands. Fade to sad music which changes to become a reel.

Scene 5

The Glasgow Fair some months later. The stall holders setting up. The acrobats, stiltwalkers etc are practising. The stallholder who arrested Geddes in the opening scene is setting up his ale stall. He watches one of the acrobats trying out some new contortion.

STALLHOLDER: **(to acrobat)** Hey . . . are you no' feart you stey lik' that?

The acrobat makes a rude sign and carries on. ALAN GEDDES strolls on. He recognises the stallholder and strides over.

GEDDES: Hey remember me!

STALLHOLDER: **(warningly)** Now I dinna want ony trouble fae you, Geddes!

GEDDES: **(sneering)** Oh you're a brave man noo withoot your pike.

STALLHOLDER: Wha says I'm withoot it? **(He lifts it from below the counter.)** Hae you no heard? The bailies an the toon cooncil of Glesca revivit the auld statute. It wis read oot the morn by tuck of drum. **(Quotes.)** 'Every stall holder must have in readiness yin halbert, jacket and steel bonnet for the eschewing of such inconvenientis as may happen'. There's a ten pun fine for no bein' preparit. **(Smiles with a hint of menace.)** So you see Geddes, I'm a' ready, but somehow I'm no anticipatin' ony trouble.

GEDDES: **(falsely affable)** Weel you'll no get ony fae me. Last year wis just a wee misunderstandin' you ken. Nae hard feelings.

He holds out his hand. The STALLHOLDER takes it and shakes it.

STALLHOLDER: We'll drink to that . . . on me.

He pours two jugs of ale and hands one to GEDDES.

GEDDES: Your health.

They drink. GEDDES drains his. Throws down money.

STALLHOLDER: We'll hae anither twa on me. **(The STALLHOLDER fills up the jugs again.)** Aye I'm sorry aboot last year. Whit happint to you in the finish?

GEDDES: I was pit in the jougs for three days. Kept in the Tolbooth jail for twa months and fineit eight pounds.

STALLHOLDER: I wis only obeyin orders you ken. I didnae want to hae to keep the Fair but the Deacon o' Crafts says I had to take ma turn. I'd hae been in there instead o' you if I hadnae agreed.

GEDDES: I'll forgie ye if you wet my thrapple again.

STALLHOLDER: Oh I think I might manage that. **(Looks around.)** I'll join you . . . since ma good wife's no here to see it. She doesna tak ower kindly to me drinkin' the profits.

GEDDES: Women! They're nothin' but trouble! That Janet Douglas cost me dear last Fairtime. Nae profit and the tinsell o' ma freedom.

STALLHOLDER: Weel at last you're gettin' your own back on that yin.

GEDDES: Whit do you mean?

STALLHOLDER: Hae you no heard? It's her turn to cool her heels in the Tolbooth jile.

GEDDES: Janet Douglas? In the Tolbooth?

STALLHOLDER: Aye . . . she's been there these twa months past, awaitin deportation to His Majesty's colonies.

GEDDES: Janet Douglas. Weel, weel, whit wis the charge?

STALLHOLDER: I'm nae quite sure, whit this particular yin was. She wis wantit for a number o' crimes, apparently.

GEDDES: Wha telt you this?

STALLHOLDER: Ma neeber George Smythe. He's the keeper o' the Tolbooth clock.

A woman, BETSY is struggling to put up her stall nearby.

BETSY: **(sarcasticly)** Wid yin o' you gallant gentlemen gie me a haun wi' this.

GEDDES move reluctantly over. The STALLHOLDER joins him. They lift up the frame for her.

BETSY: Well thank you, gentlemen. Chivalry's nae deid efter a'.

STALLHOLDER: I'm sorry Betsy. We didnae see you there.

BETSY: Nae wonder, you were bletherin awa there like twa auld fish wifies. I'll wager some puir sod's lugs wis burnin'.

STALLHOLDER: We were just talkin' aboot Janet Douglas. You mind her? The young lassie wha worked wi Geddes here last year? Did the thocht readin' act?

BETSY: **(relishing)** Mind her? Huh! I could tell you a thing or twa about that yin?

GEDDES: **(very interested)** Oh, aye? Whit aboot her?

BETSY: Weel ma man usit tae drive the coach through tae Edinburgh.

STALLHOLDER: **(laughing)** Aye, until he was found drunk in charge o' a team o' cuddies.

BETSY: **(sharply, annoyed)** Do you want tae hear this or no?

STALLHOLDER: Sorry, Betsy . . . I'm aw lugs.

While BETSY is talking and other stallholders gather, the backcloth slowly starts to turn red. They do not notice it at first.

BETSY: Weel ma man says in the spring o' last year he was drivin the coach through Edinburgh when he saw Janet Douglas been whippit through the streets.

GEDDES: A public floggin'?

BETSY: Aye.

STALLHOLDER: Did he find oot why?

BETSY: **(disgusted)** Och you ken ma man. He's got nae curiousity. Said he askit the man next to him but he wis a stranger lik' himself. If that had been me. I'd have spiered till I fun' oot.

STALLHOLDER: She's a mystery richt enough that yin.

BETSY: I aye thocht she wis a strange buddy. How did you come to work wi' her, Geddes?

GEDDES: I met her doon at the Borders. She wis beggin' on the road. Tryin' to get back hame as I understood it.

BETSY: You mean she's English?

GEDDES: Aye, I think so.

BETSY: **(vehemently)** That explains it!

The sky (ie the backcloth) is now bright red. The wind machine starts up. The music in the background increases in volume. The stallholders turn round in alarm, and start to mutter.

GEDDES: Whit's goin on?

BETSY: Look at the sky?

STALLHOLDER: Thon's a fire!

The cry of fire goes through the crowd onstage. A man runs on wearing jacket halbert and steel bonnet.

MAN: **(agitated)** Quick . . . all o' ye. Get oot o' here. The hale toon's on fire?

GEDDES: Whit?

MAN: There's hunner's o' hooses and shops ableeze. It's comin' this wey. Hurry!

A woman runs on.

WOMAN: Glesca's ableeze! You better get oot o' here.

BETSY starts to gather her stuff as do the others.

BETSY: Whit happint?

WOMAN: I dinna ken. I think it startit in the Candleriggs, but wi a' that tallow it's spreadin fast. The jile's aw but destroyit.

GEDDES: **(starts)** Whit? The Tolbooth?

WOMAN: Aye the flames have reachit the clock tower.

MAN: **(bitterly)** Aye . . . and the toonfowk let the prisoners awa.

WOMAN: If it had been left to him they'd aw ha been roastit. We could hear them screamin. Whit were we supposed to dae?

The wind rises.

MAN: God almighty. The wind's chynging. It's comin' here fast. Get the hell oota here, all of ye, quick!

They all start running off. GEDDES stands transfixed. He is alone onstage. The wind gathers force. The armed man runs back on.

MAN: For the love of God Geddes, move!

GEDDES stands motionless looking up in the other direction, his gaze fixed. The man runs over to him grabbing him by the arm.

MAN: Whit's wrang wi' you man? Whit are you lookin' at?

(GEDDES doesn't answer.) Come on, man. The fire's comin' this wey! **(The man starts to run off again.)** Come on!

He shakes his head resignedly and runs off. GEDDES continues to look up. The light begins to fade on him and comes slowly up on a different slightly raised level. We see what he has been looking at. JANET DOUGLAS is standing there, quite still. Very slowly she gives her strange enigmatic smile. Only she is lit.

There is a very slow blackout.

The End